ASK THE
CONSTITUTION

Do Immigrants Have the Right to Come to the United States?

Kathryn Ohnaka

Enslow Publishing
101 W. 23rd Street
Suite 240
New York, NY 10011
USA

enslow.com

Published in 2020 by Enslow Publishing, LLC.
101 W. 23rd Street, Suite 240, New York, NY 10011

Library of Congress Cataloging-in-Publication Data

Names: Ohnaka, Kathryn, author.
Title: Do immigrants have the right to come to the United States? / Kathryn Ohnaka.
Description: New York, NY : Enslow Publishing, 2020. | Series: Ask the constitution | Includes bibliographical references and index. | Audience: Grades 5–8.
Identifiers: LCCN 2018047376| ISBN 9781978507111 (library bound) | ISBN 9781978508439 (pbk.)
Subjects: LCSH: Emigration and immigration law—United States—Juvenile literature.
Classification: LCC KF4819.85 .O366 2020 | DDC 342.7308/2—dc23
LC record available at https://lccn.loc.gov/2018047376

Printed in the United States of America

To Our Readers: We have done our best to make sure all website addresses in this book were active and appropriate when we went to press. However, the author and the publisher have no control over and assume no liability for the material available on those websites or on any websites they may link to. Any comments or suggestions can be sent by email to customerservice@enslow.com.

Photo Credits: Cover and p. 1 top, interior pages background (Constitution) Jack R Perry Photography/Shutterstock.com, (immigrants) Andrew Lichtenstein/Corbis News/Getty Images; p. 7 MPI/Hulton Fine Art Collection/Getty Images; p. 9 Charles Haire/Shutterstock.com; p. 10 gary718/Shutterstock.com; pp. 13, 16 Everett Historical/Shutterstock.com; p. 15 Buyenlarge/Archive Photos/Getty Images; p. 20 Chris Hondros/Getty Images; p. 23 Photo_Grapher/Shutterstock.com; p. 24 Diego G Diaz/Shutterstock.com; p. 27 Prazis Images/Shutterstock.com; p. 28 nsf/Alamy Stock Photo; p. 31 Library of Congress Prints and Photographs Division; p. 34 Digital First Media/Orange County Register/Getty Images; p. 37 © AP Images; p. 38 Pacific Press/LightRocket/Getty Images; cover, interior pages (paper scroll) Andrey_Kuzmin/Shutterstock.com.

Contents

Introduction

I t's always been a struggle. Since the dawn of the American government, immigrants from all over the world have tried to come to the United States. Some were welcomed with open arms, some with protests. The argument about immigrants, especially Muslim and Latino immigrants, rages on even today.

On September 24, 2017, President Donald Trump signed the third version of the Muslim ban, an act that says certain people from Iran, Libya, Somalia, Syria, Yemen, and North Korea may not obtain visas to travel to the United States. The ban was meant to reduce the number of immigrants entering the United States from these countries. President Trump and his supporters said this will reduce acts of terrorism; opponents say it discriminates against people who practice Islam and that all immigrants have the right to enter the United States.

The ban refuses entry to people who want to come live in the United States but who have not been here before and have never been residents. The ban was challenged multiple times, and on June 26, 2018, the Supreme Court of the United States ruled that under the Immigration and Nationality Act, the president's ban would remain and that this ban would protect the interests of the United States.[1] People continue to protest and challenge the ban, claiming it is unconstitutional and that immigrants are being deprived of their right to freedoms of speech and religion, and the right to seek happiness.

There are many reasons people might want to come to the United States. They might be escaping a war, a natural disaster, violence in their

community, or a tyrannical government. They might be starving or seeking medical care they can't get in their country. They might be coming to meet family that's already here. They might be seeking better lives for their children. They need to arrive here in order to begin the process of getting a visa or green card, which can take years. However, some of them realize upon arrival that the process is halted due to a ban or hold. Imagine the frustration they feel! Yet they continue on in hopes of a better life.

Immigrants of many nationalities have often faced bans like these throughout history. European, African, and Chinese immigrants were challenged and even banned from entry in the past, as people argued that these people would steal jobs or destroy culture, or that they were not truly Americans. Repeatedly, these bans have been discussed and overturned, and the Constitution was amended to allow immigrants to stay. Today, the same battles are fought about Latino and Middle Eastern immigrants.

From the earliest Pilgrims to the immigrants today, people have wanted to come to the United States to escape terrible governments, to enjoy freedoms America provides, and to seek out a new life. Let's take a look at immigrants in America throughout history and examine the challenges they faced in the past and face today, as well as the ways the Constitution changes to meet their needs.

1

The Constitution

When the earliest immigrants, the Pilgrims, arrived in America, they were seeking freedom from King Charles I of England. They wanted to practice their own religion, be free of foreign taxes and laws, and create their own government and way of life. Each state created its own set of laws, but it was too difficult to run the country that way. After the Revolutionary War, America declared its independence, and a group called the framers came together to create the country's Constitution. Most states sent people to be framers; some of the more well-known framers included Benjamin Franklin, George Washington, and Alexander Hamilton.

Building the Constitution

The framers worked together to create the Constitution, and then each state had to approve it. It was ratified on June 21, 1788. The Constitution provides the basic framework and laws for America's government. It is the supreme law of the land, which overrides state and city laws. It states that the government must be split into three branches, in order to provide balance. It outlines how the government may collect taxes and revenue, and how voters can influence the laws. Most important, it states that the government is there to protect the people and that the Constitution forms a contract between the people and their government.[1] People have the

George Washington, Alexander Hamilton, and Thomas Jefferson each played a critical role in the development of the United States Constitution.

right to change the Constitution to meet their needs and provide greater protections as they see fit. These changes are called amendments.

According to Article V of the Constitution, amendments are created when Congress proposes a change and votes to approve it with a two-thirds majority vote in both the House of Representatives and the Senate or by a constitutional convention called for by two-thirds of the state legislatures. Eventually, the Constitution gained twenty-seven amendments, which affect a wide variety of rights. The Constitution originally granted rights only to male, white landowners. Over time, rights such as voting and citizenship were granted to people of all races and genders.

The Bill of Rights

The first ten amendments are called the Bill of Rights. Originally written by James Madison, the amendments were created to protect the liberties of the people. The amendments protect freedom of speech and press; the right to bear arms; the right for people to have their homes protected from search and seizure and from being used as soldiers' quarters; and the right to a jury trial and to be free of cruel and unusual punishments. It also says that states may make their own laws as long as they do not conflict with the Constitution.[2]

Many immigrants come to the United States because of the rights guaranteed by the Constitution, and in particular, four of the amendments are key for immigrants. The First Amendment says that all people have the right to freedom of speech, meaning they may say anything they like without the government punishing them. It says that all people have the right to their own religion and that the government may not promote one religion over another. It guarantees that people may assemble and protest without government interference. Finally, it protects freedom of the press, which means that people may print or broadcast their opinions without the government censoring them. Many immigrants who come to the United

Were Immigrants Always Covered by the Constitution?

Immigrants were not covered in the original Constitution. In the original documents, rights were afforded to white, European male landowners only, and only from certain countries. As more people began to come in from new countries, the government had to decide how to integrate them. Immigrants gained rights such as voting, due process, and citizenship from the First, Sixth, and Fourteenth Amendments. It took many years and arguments for immigrants to be considered "people" under the law.

States want these freedoms, and once they are on American soil they are allowed to have them.

The Fifth and Sixth Amendments are also key for immigrants. They grant the right to due process, which is the right to a trial, the right to have a lawyer, and to be protected from unusual punishments, such as unreasonable prison sentences. That means any immigrant who enters the country, whether legally or illegally, has the right to have a trial and have their case heard, and argue that they should be allowed to stay.[3]

Finally, the Fourteenth Amendment, which came later in 1868, is vital for many immigrants. It states that any person born on American soil is a citizen. Families of a child born in the United States have a much higher chance of becoming naturalized citizens.[4]

The Bill of Rights contains the first ten amendments to the United States Constitution. They establish specific rights of the individual.

"Give me your tired, your poor, your huddled masses yearning to breathe free, the wretched refuse of your teeming shore. Send these, the homeless, tempest-tossed to me. I lift my lamp beside the golden door!" Emma Lazarus wrote the poem engraved on the Statue of Liberty.

Acts

Another set of laws can be created by Congress called acts. Acts differ from amendments because they are not part of the Constitution, yet they are still laws. Acts often have time periods attached to them, so they can expire. They can also be modified by the government if they are not working or if circumstances change. Amendments have occasionally been reworded to include people of other races or genders, but the core idea doesn't change. Acts, however, change often, and can be cancelled. Acts such as the Immigration and Nationality Act of 1965, the Immigration Reform Act in 1986, and the 1996 Illegal Immigration Reform and Immigrant Responsibility Act affect our laws today.

The Constitution and its amendments grant a wide variety of freedoms and protections that are very appealing to immigrants from all over the world. Though some of our laws make it difficult to enter the country, people continue to do so in an attempt to access safer living conditions, freedom from oppression, and freedom from tragedies in their own countries.

A History of Immigrants in the United States

Look around you. Look at your family and friends, the things you own, and where you live. Think about your town and all of the things you love. Would you be willing to pack a few of those things into a suitcase, get on a boat, and sail to a country you've never seen to start a new life? Many people in history made that decision in the hopes of a new and better life, or to escape tragedy.

The Earliest Immigrants

As early as the 1500s, people from France, England, and Spain began to explore North America, establishing colonies in the 1600s. Many of these explorers came seeking gold and land, but inhabiting the land was difficult. In 1620, the first group of Pilgrims arrived, seeking religious freedom and hoping to begin their own colony away from the restrictive religious laws in England. Within the next twenty years, 20,000 Puritans, a religious group, came to settle on the East Coast.

More settlers came from Europe to seek jobs and land, but the trip was difficult and expensive. Many of the people sent over from Europe were criminals that were sent over to work as servants as part of their punishment.

Jean Leon Gerome Ferris painted this idyllic scene of the first Thanksgiving—but were things so serene when the Pilgrims came to the New World?

Criminals weren't the only people brought against their will. African people were captured, sold into slavery, and brought to the colonies unwillingly. There were 7,000 of them by the late 1600s, and by the time the Constitution was written, there were estimated to be around 700,000 slaves in North America. They were not considered immigrants or citizens under the law, and were therefore afforded no rights under the Constitution when it was written.[1]

When the Americans declared independence from England and created the United States of America, the bulk of the immigrants were European, mostly from England, and slaves. After that, immigration levels slowed, and the people living in the United States worked to create their own colonies and culture, and to define their government. Each state regulated its own immigration, but the rules were not clearly defined.

The Early 1800s

Immigration to the United States increased around 1815. A massive number of immigrants came from Europe, especially from Ireland, where there was a massive famine. Irish immigrants came to America hoping to find jobs and food. The Irish made up about half of the new immigrants. A great many German immigrants arrived as well and created settlements in the Midwest.[2]

Between 1845 and 1854, 2.9 million immigrants entered the country. Many American citizens objected to the Irish immigrants, both because of their need for government services and due to their Catholic faith. As more European groups moved to the United States, the anti-immigrant sentiment began to rise, especially in regard to religious ideas.

A secret society called the "Know-nothing Party" tried to slow immigration of Catholic immigrants.[3] It created a new political party called the American Party, which ran on anti-immigrant and anti-Catholic platforms. Though the party didn't last long, the movement was very strong. Members were vocal about deporting immigrants to protect their culture and lifestyle. The idea that immigrants threaten the way of life of native-born people is called nativism, and it's a view that is still held by some today.

As people moved into new territories, the need for railroads appeared, especially during the California Gold Rush in the 1850s. Asian immigrants began to arrive to build railroads, and anti-immigrant sentiment grew much stronger as Americans feared that the waves of Catholic and Asian immigration would reduce their jobs and land, and disrupt their culture.

Nativism continued to flourish during this time, resulting in the Naturalization Act of 1870, which allowed only immigrants from Europe and Africa to become citizens, excluding Asian immigrants. There was also the Alien Contract Labor Law of 1885, which prevented companies from bringing over immigrants by promising jobs. This strengthened American labor unions by limiting the number of immigrant workers and limited immigration because only immigrants who could pay for themselves could come over.[4] The law got stronger with the 1882 Chinese Exclusion Act. The laws were difficult to enforce, so the Bureau of Immigration was established in 1891 to decide how to deal with immigrants.

Railroads changed access to America completely, allowing more people to travel to more places. Railroads were often built by Chinese immigrants and the enslaved.

1882 Chinese Exclusion Act

Many laborers came from China to work in agriculture and industry, and were especially known for building railroad lines. Americans were afraid they would lose their jobs to Chinese laborers and worried they would "destroy their culture." California began to require that Chinese people carry special licenses. In 1882, President Hayes signed the Chinese Exclusion Act, which said no new Chinese immigrants could come into the country for ten years and those already here must have a special license. The act was renewed several times. Relations between America and China soured. The act was repealed in 1943.[5]

The 1900s

On January 1, 1892, the immigration station on Ellis Island opened, and over the next sixty-two years, around 12 million immigrants passed through. More people came from all over Europe, particularly during World War I. Toward the end of World War I, the first "Red Scare," which was a paranoia about Communists attempting to corrupt American politics, caused immigrants suspected of Communist ties to be detained and hundreds to be deported.[6]

The government enacted the National Origins Quota System, or the Immigration Act of 1924. It allotted a set number of visas, and once they were given out, no more immigrants could enter the country for the year. The visas were not issued to Asian immigrants at all. Immigrants also had to pass a literacy test.

The next major change was the Immigration and Nationality Act of 1952, also known as the McCarran-Walter Act, which continued the quota system while officially ending Asian exclusion.[7] Instead, it created a system of merit, where people with special skills or family in the country would

Ellis Island in New York was a major entry point to the United States; people were often held in pens as they awaited inspection and entry.

be prioritized for visas, as well as increasing the number of visas. The vast majority of the visas were still given to European immigrants, with a very small number of visas allotted for Asians. The act did provide some helpful new rules, however: it allowed spouses with alien husbands to immigrate without worrying about the visa quota.

The quota system ended with the Immigration and Nationality Act of 1965, also called the Hart-Celler Act. Immigrants from Southern and Eastern Europe were allotted fewer visas under the quota system and said the system discriminated against them. President John Kennedy agreed and pressed Congress to reform immigration. The new act in 1965 removed the quotas and prioritized relatives of US citizens or permanent residents, refugees of violence or unrest in their own country, and people with skills useful for the United States. Family reunification became a major goal, and immigrants' families began to immigrate as well. Immigrants shifted from being primarily European to include Asian and South American immigrants.[8]

This act continues to impact us today, as this is the main system we still use. The Immigration Reform Act in 1986 added amnesty for illegal immigrants and created more pathways to legal immigration.

In 1996, Congress passed the Illegal Immigration Reform and Immigrant Responsibility Act. This act created penalties for illegal immigrants if they commit a crime or overstay their visa, or are in the United States without a visa. These immigrants can be deported if they are caught.[9] In 2002, the Homeland Security Act of 2002 created the Department of Homeland Security (DHS), which took over many of the duties of the immigration bureau, and these are the laws we have in place today.

3

The Fourteenth Amendment

When President Abraham Lincoln gave the Emancipation Proclamation on January 1, 1863, it created a unique problem for the United States. The Proclamation declared that all slaves were free. However, how would the government classify them? They had been brought to the United States unwillingly, so they didn't qualify as immigrants. Because there were several generations between the current population and the original slaves, they had no way to return to Africa. The government began to question how to integrate them into the general population. Were they citizens?

Not initially. The Thirteenth Amendment abolished slavery, but it was hard to enforce, so in 1866, Congress created the Civil Rights Act. It states that "all persons born in the United States hereby declared to be citizens of the United States," however, it did not include Native Americans.[1]

About two months later, the government decided the law needed to be even stronger, drafting the Fourteenth Constitutional Amendment. It was designed to protect the civil rights of African Americans, confer them citizenship, and punish the Confederate states. President Andrew Johnson

BY THE PRESIDENT OF THE UNITED STATES

A Proclamation

Whereas, on the twenty-second day of September, in the year of our Lord one thousand eight hundred and sixty-two, a proclamation was issued by the President of the United States, containing, among other things, the following, to wit:

"That on the first day of January, in the year of our Lord one thousand eight hundred and sixty-three, all persons held as slaves within any State or designated part of a State, the people whereof shall then be in rebellion against the United States, shall be then, thenceforward, and forever, free; and the Executive government of the United States, including the military and naval authority thereof, will recognize and maintain the freedom of such persons, and will do no act or acts to repress such persons, or any of them, in any efforts they may make for their actual freedom.

"That the Executive will, on the first day of January aforesaid, by proclamation, designate the States and parts of States, if any, in which the people thereof, respectively, shall then be in rebellion against the United States; and the fact that any State, or the people thereof, shall on that day be, in good faith, represented in the Congress

The Emancipation Proclamation freed African Americans from slavery, but the United States government had no immediate idea how to classify the freed people.

objected to the amendment, but he was vetoed by the House and Senate, who felt the amendment was vital to enforcing these new ideas.

The first section of the Fourteenth Amendment states, "All persons born or naturalized in the United States and subject to the jurisdiction thereof, are citizens of the United States and of the State wherein they reside." This means that anyone born on American soil is automatically a citizen. It also grants that all people born in the United States are guaranteed their rights under the Constitution and the Bill of Rights, and are all guaranteed due process, or the right to a trial.[2] It also includes an equal protection clause, which means that states have to govern people equally. It was designed to keep the Confederate states from discriminating against African Americans as a whole. It meant that the laws had to be equal, but discriminatory laws were acceptable.[3]

This still allowed for discrimination against individuals, such as under the "Separate but Equal" laws, but it said that the courts could not discriminate against people because of their race. This is also why it remained acceptable to ban certain sets of immigrants; immigrants wanting to come to the United States were not citizens yet and therefore afforded no

Are Women Citizens?

When the Fourteenth Amendment was created, the second portion of the amendment says only males may vote. Why, when all people born in the United States were citizens, could women not be given the same rights? Married women at the time were considered property of their husbands, not people in their own right. In 1872, in the case *Minor v. Happersett*, the Supreme Court found that women born or naturalized in the United States were American citizens under the amendment, but they were not allowed to vote.[4] Women's rights advocates later cited this amendment in their fight to vote, citing that as citizens, they should be allowed to do so.

protection. However, if they were able to enter either legally or illegally, then their child was immediately considered a citizen and therefore had protection under the law. This law is still in place today.

The Fourteenth Amendment also says that no state can "deprive any person of life, liberty, or property, without due process of law; nor deny to any person within its jurisdiction the equal protection of the laws." There is a key distinction here: "people" vs. "citizens." The amendment says "people," not citizens, are afforded rights and due process.[5] "People" is generally taken to mean those with their feet on American soil, which includes immigrants regardless of whether they entered legally or not.

This was affirmed in the 1898 case of *United States v. Wong Kim Ark*. Wong Kim Ark was born in San Francisco during the Chinese Exclusion Act to Chinese parents. He went back to China then tried to reenter the United States as a citizen. The government argued that due to the ban, he was not a citizen. However, the US Supreme Court decided that "the Fourteenth Amendment to the Constitution is not confined to the protection of citizens." This is because the Amendment says "people," and since Wong Kim Ark was born in the United States as a person, he was also a citizen.

The Fourteenth Amendment Today

That doesn't mean if a baby is born in United States, they automatically remain in the country. Some people think that if they have a baby in the United States, that they and the baby may stay in the country; these are called "anchor babies." Legally, the child has to have at least one guardian who legally lives in the United States, either a citizen or a legal alien with a visa.[6] In the case of Wong Kim Ark, his parents were living in the United States during his lifetime as legal citizens. A

Since 1868, anyone born in the United States has been considered a citizen, whether or not their parents entered the country legally. Will this remain the case?

child born in the United States to parents who are here illegally or on a tourist visa can still be deported, and their parents have no right to stay. However, since the child is a citizen, they can apply for residency as an adult later in life.

What about a child born and raised here by parents here illegally? There have been many cases of this recently. It's a difficult problem because the child is a US citizen under the Fourteenth Amendment, and therefore cannot be deported. If the parents are discovered, they can be deported, and the child goes into the foster care system or to

Barack Obama established the Deferred Action on Childhood Arrivals (DACA) immigration policy in an effort to support children who arrived in the United States illegally.

relatives if there are any legal ones available. The parents may not attempt to return until the child is twenty-one years old, and even then, it's difficult because the deported person faces penalties for being in the country illegally.[7] There is much argument about whether children born here illegally are truly citizens, despite what the amendment says, but because amendments are difficult to change, the law is unlikely to change.[8]

Children who are born in a different country and brought in illegally are not considered citizens, and it's difficult for them to become citizens.

Under Deferred Action on Childhood Arrivals (DACA), established by President Barack Obama in 2012, if they fit specific guidelines, they may apply for deferred action, which allows them to stay in the United States longer, or apply for legal citizenship. It's important to note that those who arrived as infants or young children are not automatically citizens if they weren't born in the United States and do not have constitutional protection.

The Fourteenth Amendment gives automatic citizenship and protection to everyone born on American soil and protects them from deportation. It also grants them rights under the Constitution and the Bill of Rights.

4

How Does the Bill of Rights Affect Immigration?

Meet Cristina Bebawy. A citizen of Morocco, she came to the United States for asylum, meaning she was seeking protection from her own country's government. In Morocco, she was arrested and tortured for teaching a Bible lesson. She came to the United States seeking freedom to practice her own religion. She is one of many. People are arrested in their countries for writing blogs the governments don't agree with, practicing a religion that the government doesn't approve of, having a different race or sexual orientation, or for not behaving in a way their government sees as appropriate.[1]

The Bill of Rights contains the first ten amendments of the Constitution, and some are particularly vital to immigrants coming into the United States. Many come seeking the protection the Bill of Rights provides. They are the First, Fifth, and Sixth Amendments.

The First Amendment

The First Amendment says, "Congress shall make no law respecting an establishment of religion, or prohibiting the free exercise thereof; or abridging the freedom of speech, or of the press; or the right of the people

The Fourteenth Amendment gives automatic citizenship and protection to everyone born on American soil and protects them from deportation. It also grants them rights under the Constitution and the Bill of Rights.

Wong Kim Ark was born in San Francisco during the time of the Chinese Exclusion Act, to Chinese parents. He went back to China, then tried to reenter the United States as a citizen. The government argued that due to the ban, he was not a citizen. The Supreme Court disagreed.

Is a "Person" the Same as a "Citizen?"

"We the People..." begins the Constitution. In fact, most of the amendments use this language as well. "People" refers to a human in the United States, while "citizen" refers to a person with legal American citizenship, either by being born here or going through a citizenship process. The amendments refer to people, not to citizens; therefore, all people, legal or illegal, receive the basic rights from the Constitution. This was determined by the Supreme Court in 1898 during the Wong Kim Ark case; all immigrants are "people" even if they are not citizens.

peaceably to assemble, and to petition the government for a redress of grievances." What does this mean to us today? Essentially, it protects the rights to freedom of speech, freedom of religion, freedom of the press, and freedom to assemble and protest.[2]

Freedom of speech means that you may express your opinion, either written or spoken, without punishment from the government. Yes, that includes things that others may find distasteful, such as hate speech. It means people can say anything they please. Some countries censor their people, denying them access to the internet or punishing them for speaking against the government. Some people, such as Malala Yousafzai, have been shot for daring to write blogs or give speeches that argued with the government.[3]

Freedom of religion means that the government cannot establish a religion or demand that the people practice it, but government is allowed to have prayer meetings if they choose. However, they cannot demand that the people attend or participate. Many immigrants find America appealing because they would like to practice a different religion from that of their country, or none at all.

Freedom to assemble means that any group of people may protest or march as they like without interference from the government, unless they are actively causing damage or committing violence. It means that no matter how terrible other people may think a protest is, that group still has the right to gather and protest as they see fit. To some immigrants, the ability to speak their minds without fear of punishment is very appealing.

The Fifth Amendment

The Fifth Amendment says, "No person shall be held to answer for a capital, or otherwise infamous crime, unless on a presentment or indictment of a grand jury, except in cases arising in the land or naval forces, or in the militia, when in actual service in time of war or public danger; nor shall any person be subject for the same offense to be twice put in jeopardy of life or limb; nor shall be compelled in any criminal case to be a witness against himself, nor be deprived of life, liberty, or property, without due process of law; nor shall private property be taken for public use, without just compensation."

This means that a person cannot be tried in a court unless they've been correctly indicted by the police and read their rights. They do not have to speak if they don't want to, and they cannot be forced to testify. They may not be tried twice for the same crime. In addition, they cannot be held indefinitely without a proper trial or have their property taken.

Much of this was used during the late 1800s, when Chinese immigrants were challenging the Chinese Exclusion Act.[4] Several of them challenged that their property had been seized and they had been punished unfairly, because they were being deported if they didn't carry the proper identification, even if they didn't break any laws. They said that they were being given cruel and unusual punishment. The Supreme Court ruled in *Fong Yue Ting v. United States* in 1893 that while the rights applied to people,

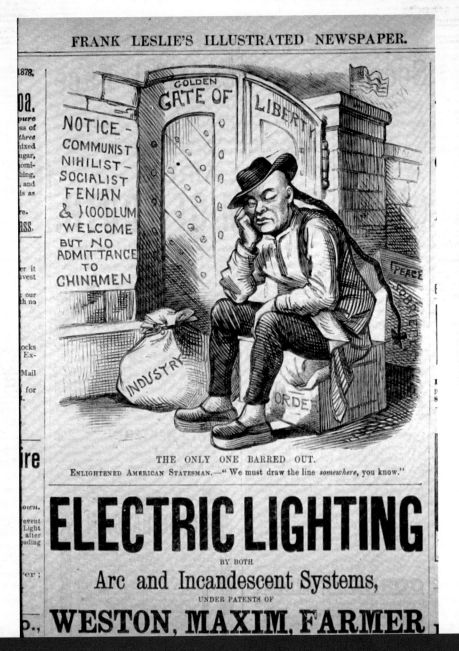

This political cartoon addresses the Chinese Exclusion Act, showing that America would allow entry to all—except one. Today, one could redraw this to show what groups being barred entry?

deportation was not a punishment, but rather a safety measure.[5] So, while people are afforded rights under the Constitution, there is some leeway in how the law is interpreted and what "punishment" might mean.

The Sixth Amendment

The Sixth Amendment says, "In all criminal prosecutions, the accused shall enjoy the right to a speedy and public trial, by an impartial jury of the state and district wherein the crime shall have been committed, which district shall have been previously ascertained by law, and to be informed of the nature and cause of the accusation; to be confronted with the witnesses against him; to have compulsory process for obtaining witnesses in his favor, and to have the assistance of counsel for his defense." This means that again, all people, whether they are citizens or not, have the right to a jury trial. They have the right to defend themselves and know who might testify against them and why.

These amendments apply to illegal immigrants also. Immigrants who enter the country illegally and are detained in the United States have the right to be properly processed by the police, not forced to testify if they don't want to, and the right to an impartial jury trial. Asylum seekers are also granted these rights.

Immigration Law Today and the Rights of Immigrants

How does someone who enters the country legally become a citizen of the United States? Can those who enter the country illegally ever be legal citizens? Let's explore some of the paths toward citizenship.

Entering the Country Legally

What does it take to become a legal citizen of the United States? Right now, most immigrants need to be sponsored by a family member, a school, or an employer. For example, if you marry a foreigner, they are required to apply for a visa, which is a document that allows them to stay in the country. Visas can be issued for family, for studying, or for work. However, some visas are only for one thing; for instance, a person may only work with a work visa.[1] Visas are also only valid for a limited time, so a student visa would only be valid until the student has their degree or for a year of school. Immigration laws currently do not allow for single countries to be discriminated against when it comes to issuing visas.[2]

If an immigrant wishes to stay for an unlimited amount of time, they can apply for a green card. A green card allows them to work and grants

Requirements for American citizenship include taking classes and learning about the Bill of Rights and Constitution. There is also a civics test about American history and the English language.

them all the rights of a citizen except for voting, being on a jury, or getting a student loan.[3]

If an immigrant wishes to become a full citizen, they must apply for citizenship. The process requires a great deal of paperwork, interviews, security screenings, and finally, a citizenship test. This is a written test about basic civics and American history, and a basic level of spoken and written English. Once the person passes the interviews and test, they take the Oath of Citizenship and are granted all of the rights of a citizen. Some countries, such as Sweden, allow for dual citizenship, meaning the person may be a citizen of both countries at the same time. Other countries, like Japan, require the person to renounce, or give up, their original citizenship. This process usually takes at least a year, sometimes decades.

Asylum seekers are special cases. They may be granted a long-term visa, but they must go through a trial first. They may then apply for a green card, which grants them a longer stay.

What Are the Rights of Illegal Immigrants?

In the 1898 case of *United States v. Wong Kim Ark*, it was ruled that immigrants are people. Therefore, even illegal immigrants are people and afforded all rights except when it comes to immigration law. In the areas of immigration law, they can be detained, though they must be given a trial before they are deported, imprisoned, freed, or granted a visa. This was challenged again in 2001; however, in the case of *Zadvydas v. Davis*, the Supreme Court ruled that "due process" of the Fourteenth Amendment applies to all aliens in the United States whose presence maybe or is "unlawful, involuntary or transitory," which reaffirms that illegal immigrants are granted rights as people.[4]

Zadvydas vs. Davis created an interesting problem. The case involved two immigrants who had committed crimes, but their countries of origin would not take them back. As such, the Supreme Court ruled that they could not be held "indefinitely" and therefore had to be released. The ruling affected several thousand immigrants who were being detained. Part of the problem was the vague language of previous laws.

The Supreme Court argued that under the Fifth Amendment, the law permits "reasonable" detention, which isn't defined, but in *Zadvydas vs. Davis* it was considered to be about six months.[5] However, the Illegal Immigration Reform and Immigrant Responsibility Act of 1996 says that detention is mandatory for illegal immigrants awaiting their trial.

Today, there is much argument within the government about how long a mandatory detention should be. By September 2018, there were about 30,000 people in detention, including asylum seekers and children, awaiting their due process.[6] The detention time is capped, but President Trump has pressed government agencies to remove the time limit and hold people indefinitely.

Trump and his team argue that detaining immigrants will reduce crime and terrorism. They cite the *Fong Yue Ting vs. United States* case as proof that they can deport people to keep the country safe. They also cite the Immigration and Nationality Act of 1952, specifically this: "In general any alien who a consular officer or the Attorney General knows, or has reasonable ground to believe, seeks to enter the United States to engage solely, principally, or incidentally in any activity a purpose of which is the opposition to, or the control or overthrow of, the Government of the United States by force, violence, or other unlawful means." Trump says that he can use this because people from the countries in his travel ban would be likely to commit crimes.

Opponents argue that the long periods of detention, which are handled by detention facilities, are detrimental to the health of the immigrants, especially children. Some detention centers are inside of prisons, and

In the summers of 2017 and 2018, the Trump administration began to detain people at the US-Mexico border, keeping refugees and immigrants in cages with no clear guidelines on what was to become of them.

Protests against Muslim bans and proposed border walls continue—and the words on the Statue of Liberty remain: "Give me your tired, your poor, your huddled masses yearning to breathe free."

The Muslim Ban: Is It Constitutional?

Presidential Proclamation 9645, also known as "the Muslim ban," was upheld by the Supreme Court in June 2018. It stops the acceptance of visa applications from Iran, Libya, North Korea, Somalia, Syria, Yemen, and some from Venezuela.[7] Most of these countries are predominately Islamic. While this doesn't ban all Muslims, it makes it difficult for many of them to seek asylum, and some are turned away at the border without a trial.[8] Some people who are attempting to enter to reunite with their families can no longer do so. Based on what you've read, is this proclamation constitutional?

families are often separated from their children. Many of the people have their belongings taken away[9] and live in crowded conditions with poor food and do not feel safe.[10] Given what you've read about the rights given to all people, are these immigrants' rights being taken away by this system?

Immigrants have the right to come to the United States, and as time goes on they will continue to do so. The freedoms granted to us will continue to draw people from all over the world in hopes of a better life. How do you think laws should change as time goes on?

Chapter Notes

Introduction

1. D'Angelo Gore and Lori Robertson, "Trump's 'Travel Ban' Doesn't Affect All Muslims," Factcheck.org, June 29, 2018, https://www.factcheck.org/2018/06/trumps-travel-ban-doesnt-affect-all-muslims/.

Chapter One. The Constitution

1. "The Constitution," http://constitutionus.com/.
2. "U.S. Constitution: Civil Rights and Liberties: Law," Immigration to the United States, http://immigrationtounitedstates.org/447-us-constitution.html.
3. "The Bill of Rights," Bill of Rights Institute, https://billofrightsinstitute.org/founding-documents/bill-of-rights/.
4. "14th Amendment," History.com, https://www.history.com/topics/black-history/fourteenth-amendment.

Chapter Two. A History of Immigrants in the United States

1. "U.S. Immigration Before 1965," History.com, September 14, 2018, https://www.history.com/topics/immigration/u-s-immigration-before-1965.
2. The Statue of Liberty-Ellis Island Foundation Inc., https://www.libertyellisfoundation.org/ellis-island-history#Policy.
3. Lorraine Boissoneault, "How the 19th-Century Know Nothing Party Reshaped American Politics," The Smithsonian.com, January 26, 2016, https://www.smithsonianmag.com/history/immigrants-conspiracies-and-secret-society-launched-american-nativism-180961915/.

4. "Alien Contract Labor Law of 1885," http://immigrationtounitedstates .org/333-alien-contract-labor-law-of-1885.html.

5. "Milestones in the History of U.S. Foreign Relations: Chinese Immigration and the Chinese Exclusion Acts," Office of the Historian, https://history.state.gov/milestones/1866-1898/chinese-immigration.

6. The Statue of Liberty-Ellis Island Foundation Inc., https://www .libertyellisfoundation.org/ellis-island-history#Policy.

7. The Office of the Historian, https://history.state.gov/milestones/1945-1952 /immigration-act.

8. "US Immigration Since 1965," History.com, August 21, 2018, https:// www.history.com/topics/immigration/us-immigration-since-1965.

9. "Illegal Immigration Reform and Immigration Responsibility Act," Legal Information Institute, https://www.law.cornell.edu/wex /illegal_immigration_reform_and_immigration_responsibility_act.

Chapter Three. The Fourteenth Amendment

1. History, Art and Archives: United States House of Representatives, Historical Highlights: the Civil Rights Act of 1866, http://history.house .gov/Historical-Highlights/1851-1900/The-Civil-Rights-Bill-of-1866/.

2. "14th Amendment," August 21, 2018, https://www.history.com/topics /black-history/fourteenth-amendment.

3. Cornell Law School: Equal Protection, https://www.law.cornell.edu /wex/equal_protection.

4. Law Day: The 14th Amendment, https://www.courierpress.com /story/opinion/2017/04/29/law-day-14th-amendment-and -immigration/100814424/.

5. Jone Johnson Lewis, "Women's Rights and the 14th Amendment," June 4, 2018, https://www.thoughtco.com/womens-rights-and-the-fourteenth-amendment-3529473.

6. Andy J. Semotiuk, "Immigration: The Myth of the 'Anchor Baby,'" Forbes .com, September 22, 2014, https://www.forbes.com/sites/andyjsemotiuk /2014/09/22/immigration-the-myth-of-the-anchor-baby/#1c336111e801.

7. Ilona Bray, "Can the Child of an Undocumented Immigrant Become a U.S. Citizen?," 2018, http://www.alllaw.com/articles/nolo/us -immigration/can-child-undocumented-immigrant-become-citizen.html.

8. Jessie Higgins, "Birthright Citizenship Applies to Children of Undocumented Immigrants," January 18, 2018, https://www .courierpress.com/story/news/2018/01/18/birthright-citizenship -applies-children-undocumented-immigrants/1014695001/.

Chapter Four. How Does the Bill of Rights Affect Immigration?

1. Miriam Jordan, "What It Takes to Get Asylum in the US," May 2, 2018, https://www.nytimes.com/2018/05/02/us/what-it-takes-to-get -asylum-us.html.

2. Richard Wolf, "What the First Amendment Protects—and What It Doesn't," USA Today, April 6, 2018, https://www.usatoday.com /story/news/politics/2018/04/06/what-first-amendment-protects -and-what-doesnt/469920002/.

3. "Malala Yousafzai Biography," March 29, 2018, https://www.biography .com/people/malala-yousafzai-21362253.

4. Daniel Fisher, "Does the Constitution Protect Non-Citizens? Judges Say Yes," Forbes.com, January 30, 2017, https://www.forbes.com

/sites/danielfisher/2017/01/30/does-the-constitution-protect-non
-citizens-judges-say-yes/#43dad26e4f1d.

5. Evan Taparata, "While the Supreme Court considers deportation policy, the roots of deportation itself come from a much earlier case," Public Radio International, June 15, 2016, https://www.pri.org /stories/2016-06-15/while-supreme-court-considers-deportation -policy-deportation-policy-has-its-roots.

Chapter Five. Immigration Law Today and the Rights of Immigrants

1. "Immigrate," US Department of State—Bureau of Consular Affairs, https://travel.state.gov/content/travel/en/us-visas/immigrate.html.

2. 8 U.S. Code § 1152 - Numerical limitations on individual foreign states, Cornell Law School, https://www.law.cornell.edu/uscode/text/8/1152.

3. "Is There a Difference Between a Visa and a Green Card?," https://www .hg.org/legal-articles/is-there-a-difference-between-a-visa-and-a-green -card-28885.

4. Linda Greenhouse, "The Supreme Court: The Issue of Confinement; Supreme Court Limits Detention in Cases of Deportable Immigrants," *New York Times*, June 29, 2001, https://www.nytimes.com/2001/06/29 /us/supreme-court-issue-confinement-supreme-court-limits -detention-cases-deportable.html.

5. Ibid.

6. The Global Detention Project, 2018, https://www.globaldetention project.org/countries/americas/united-states.

7. "Revisions to Presidential Proclamation 9645," US Department of State— Bureau of Consular Affairs, https://travel.state.gov/content/travel/en /us-visas/visa-information-resources/presidential-proclamation-archive

/june_26_supreme_court_decision_on_presidential_proclamation9645
.html.

8. D'Angelo Gore and Lori Robertson, "Trump's 'Travel Ban' Doesn't Affect All Muslims," Factcheck.org, June 29, 2018, https://www .factcheck.org/2018/06/trumps-travel-ban-doesnt-affect-all-muslims/.

9. Dagmar R. Myslinska, "Living Conditions in Immigration Detention Centers," 2018, https://www.nolo.com/legal-encyclopedia/living -conditions-immigration-detention-centers.html.

10. "'Traumatic' or 'summer camp'? Officials offer different views on family separation," CBS/AP, 2018, https://www.cbsnews.com/news /top-ice-official-says-detention-centers-like-summer-camp/.

Glossary

act A statute or law made by a legislative body such as Congress. Acts can expire or be changed more easily than amendments.

alien A foreign person who is not a citizen; they can be legally or illegally living in the country.

amendment An article added to the Constitution that causes it to change.

amnesty When a person is pardoned for a criminal offense, such as speaking out against another government, and allowed to stay in the country.

citizen A native or naturalized person who has full protection of the laws of the country.

Constitution The document for all legal authority in the United States, established in 1789.

deportation Removing someone from the country and sending them back to their own country.

detention When the government holds someone in custody, often to wait for a trial.

green card A permit that lets a person legally live and work permanently in the United States.

illegal immigrant An alien who enters or lives in the country without a permit or overstays a legal permit.

immigrant Any person who comes to live in a country permanently.

nativism The idea that immigrants threaten the lifestyle, culture, or ideas of native-born people.

ratify To approve or give formal consent to something, making it valid or legal.

visa A certificate or stamp in a person's passport that allows them to legally stay in a country.

Further Reading

Books

Grande, Reyna. *The Distance Between Us*. New York, NY: Aladdin, Simon and Schuster, 2016.

Guerrero, Diane, and Erica Moroz. *My Family Divided: One Girl's Journey of Home, Loss, and Hope*. New York, NY: Henry Holt and Co., 2018.

Khan, Khizr. *This Is Our Constitution: Discover America with a Gold Star Father*. New York, NY: Knopf Books for Young Readers, Penguin Random House, 2017.

Websites

The Constitution for Kids

www.usconstitution.net/constkids4.html

A kid-friendly resource for the Constitution and its amendments.

Library of Congress: Immigration

www.loc.gov/teachers/classroommaterials/presentationsandactivities/ presentations/immigration/index.html

Explore immigration from countries all over the world!

Scholastic.com: Immigration: Stories of Yesterday and Today

teacher.scholastic.com/activities/immigration/

Explore Ellis Island, hear immigrants' stories, and find helpful charts about immigration over time.

Index